Papier-Mâché

Written and Illustrated by
Renée Schwarz

KIDS CAN PRESS

To Pippa, Sophie and Alex
for their ideas and sticky-fingers help

Kids Can Press acknowledges the support of the Government of Ontario, through the Ontario Media Development Corporation's Ontario Book Initiative, and the Government of Canada, through the BPIDP, for our publishing activity.

Published in Canada by
Kids Can Press Ltd.
29 Birch Avenue
Toronto, ON M4V 1E2

Published in the U.S. by
Kids Can Press Ltd.
2250 Military Road
Tonawanda, NY 14150

www.kidscanpress.com

Edited by Laurie Wark
Designed by Karen Powers
Printed in Hong Kong, China, by Wing King Tong Company Limited

The hardcover of this edition is smyth sewn casebound.
The paperback edition of this book is limp sewn with a drawn-on cover.

CM 00 0 9 8 7 6 5 4 3 2
CM PA 00 0 9 8 7 6 5 4 3 2

Canadian Cataloguing in Publication Data

Schwarz, Renée
  Papier-mâché

(Kids can do it)
ISBN 1-55074-833-5 (bound)   1-55074-727-4 (pbk.)

1. Papier-mâché — Juvenile literature. I. Title. II. Series.

TT871.S38 2000   j745.54'2   C99-932108-0

Kids Can Press is a *Corus*™ Entertainment company

Contents

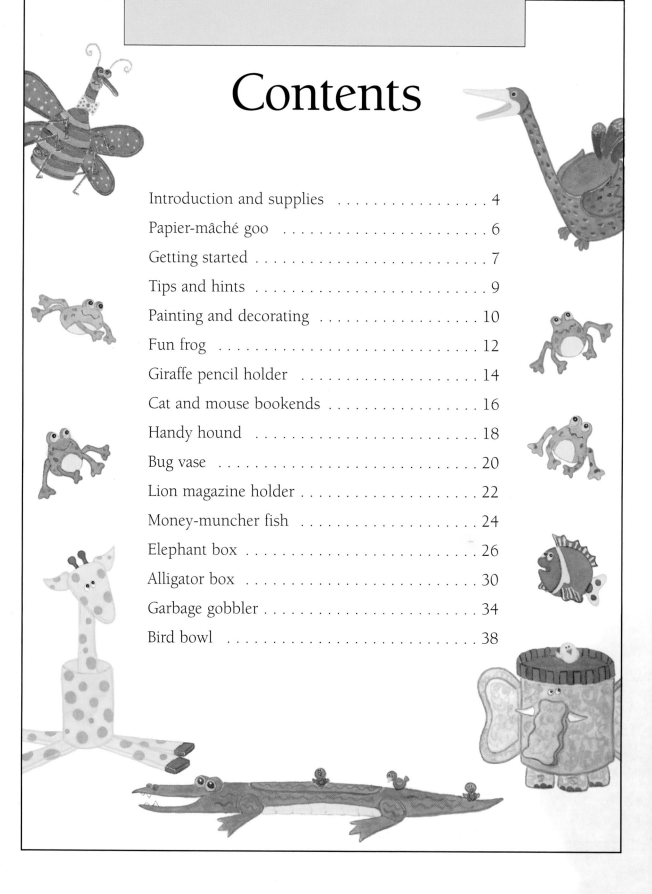

Introduction

You can start right now — all it takes is some newspaper, flour and water! Papier-mâché is a craft anyone can do, to make just about anything. Simple or complicated, large or small, papier-mâché objects are layers of paper and paste — that's all. Many things have been made from papier-mâché, from tiny, delicate jewelry to huge, strong pieces of furniture and, at one time, even houses.

The projects in this book are useful and fun to make. Most take three or four days to finish, but you work only an hour or so a day. Use the ideas and techniques as guides to make whatever you want. You can transform any old box or container into some crazy papier-mâché creature.

SUPPLIES

The materials you need for papier-mâché can be found around the house, some just waiting to be thrown out. Refer back to these pages when gathering your supplies.

Newspaper

Newspaper is the best paper to use — make sure everyone has read it before tearing it up! Other types of paper can also be used. Experiment with what's handy.

Flour

You'll need flour and water to make papier-mâché paste called goo. See the recipe on page 6.

Boxes

Most of the projects in this book are based on cardboard boxes and forms. Start saving paper rolls, ice cream and frozen juice containers, and detergent, juice and shoe boxes.

Scissors and craft knife

You will need scissors and sometimes a craft knife to cut out shapes. Ask an adult to help you with a craft knife, and protect your work surface with another piece of cardboard.

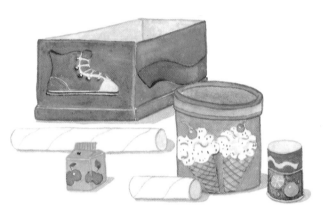

Glue and tape

For joining pieces together, you need white glue and masking tape. A hot-glue gun can be used with an adult's help.

Cardboard

Two types of cardboard are used — thin cardboard, which cereal and tissue boxes are made of, and heavier corrugated cardboard, which packing boxes are made from. You will often use two or three layers of cardboard so that the shapes are stronger and more three-dimensional.

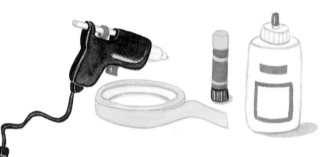

Sandpaper

You'll need medium or fine sandpaper to prepare the cardboard for papier-mâché and the papier-mâché for paint.

Papier-mâché goo

Most papier-mâché pastes are made with flour and water and are very liquid. By cooking the flour-and-water mixture, you get a thicker, gooier paste that uses less flour, dries more quickly and is less messy than other recipes.

YOU WILL NEED

- 125 mL (½ c.) white flour
- 500 mL (2 c.) water
- a saucepan
- a spoon
- a plastic container or glass bowl

1 In the saucepan, stir the water and flour together until there are no lumps.

2 Ask an adult to cook the mixture on medium heat, stirring constantly until the mixture starts to bubble. It should be thick and creamy. Cook for ten more seconds, then pour the goo into a plastic or glass container.

3 Let the goo cool a few minutes, then peel off the skin that has formed on top. When covered, leftover goo will keep for about three days in the fridge. If it starts to smell sour or turn pink or green, throw it out.

Getting started

SETTING UP

Tape a plastic bag down to cover your work surface. Cover yourself with an old T-shirt and keep a rag handy to wipe your hands. Papier-mâché can be messy, but it washes up with soap and water. Prepare a batch of papier-mâché goo (see page 6).

RIPPING NEWSPAPER

Newspaper tears easily into straight strips if you rip it lengthwise. Tear strips about 2.5 cm x 15 cm (1 in. x 6 in.). Even when covering a big surface, use this size because the strips overlap and make your piece stronger. For small parts or for around curves, you may need strips about 1 cm x 5 cm (½ in. x 2 in.) or smaller.

APPLYING GOO

Hold a strip of newspaper in the palm of your hand, dip a finger in the goo, and wipe it on the strip. Cover the strip well, but not too thickly; squish or wipe off any lumps.

Instructions continue on the next page ☞

LAYERING STRIPS

Apply the papier-mâché strips in the same direction — up and down or sideways. Overlap the edges of the strips. Once the form is covered, add another layer. Place the strips of this layer in the opposite direction, so that you can see what section you still need to cover.

For a long thin part, such as a neck or a leg, wind a strip around the piece at an angle. Wind the next strip around so that it fills the gaps.

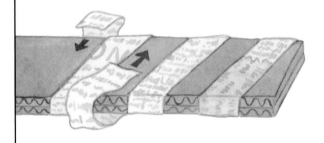

Add extra strips where parts are attached, for example an ear to the head.

HOW MANY LAYERS?

The number of layers of papier-mâché you need depends on the project. If you are covering a sturdy cardboard form, four layers are usually enough. The projects that are molded, or that get their shape from a form that is later removed, may need at least ten layers of papier-mâché to be solid. The more layers, the stronger it will be. If there are any soft spots, add a few extra layers to those areas.

DRYING

After applying four or five layers of papier-mâché, let your piece dry completely before continuing. Too many layers at once take too long to dry thoroughly and may get moldy. Papier-mâché often takes at least one day to dry. If it feels cool, it is not quite dry. Papier-mâché dries fastest in a sunny window or near a heat vent. Place your piece on a rack or prop it on empty tissue boxes so that the air can circulate, or turn it upside down so that the bottom dries.

You can shape your papier-mâché form by gently bending it before it dries. Hold it in place with an elastic if necessary.

TIPS AND HINTS

Sanding

Some cardboard containers have a waxy or shiny coating. Sand them so that the papier-mâché will stick properly and air bubbles won't appear later. If you want your papier-mâché to be very smooth, lightly sand it once it is dry before painting.

Making forms

For projects that are based on cardboard shapes, make your form as solid as possible. When adding pieces or crumpled paper to build up the shape, tape them down well. The more finished your form is, the fewer layers of papier-mâché you'll need to add.

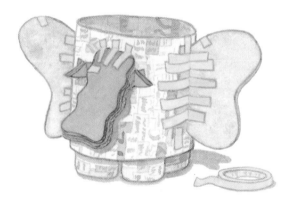

Mistakes

The great thing about papier-mâché is that you can easily fix mistakes. Just cut off parts, add on others, then cover with a few more layers of papier-mâché. Finished pieces often have small lumps and bumps that give them character and make them unique.

Adding on parts

To attach parts that stick out, such as ears or fins, make the part 1 cm (½ in.) longer than needed. You need two layers for these parts. Once you have cut out the first part, trace around it and cut out the second shape.

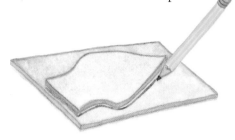

Glue the shapes together, leaving the extra 1 cm (½ in.) unglued.

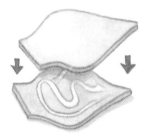

When the glue is dry, fold out the unglued area to make a **T** shape.

These flaps will be glued and taped onto the form.

Painting and decorating

Once the papier-mâché part of the project is done, the fun of decorating begins. On these pages, you'll find techniques for painting your project. Paint supplies are available at craft and art supply stores. Refer back to this section when you are ready to paint.

PRIMER

You'll need a white primer, such as gesso or white latex paint, to prepare the surface before painting. Paint your piece with a coat or two of primer so that the print doesn't show through. (Colored newspaper ink, especially red, is hard to cover, so do not use any in the final layer of papier-mâché.) You can also use blank newsprint or white paper for the last layer, instead of a primer.

PAINT AND BRUSHES

You will need paint, a few inexpensive paintbrushes in different sizes, plastic lids for palettes, and a water jar for cleaning the brushes. Acrylic paint is best because it dries quickly, it doesn't wash or flake off, and the colors are bright and strong. Acrylic paint also cleans up easily with soap and water, but once it is dry, it will not wash out of your paintbrushes or clothes. Other paints, such as gouache, tempera and poster paints, may be used. You can protect these paints with a coat of acrylic varnish, but always test first to be sure the paint doesn't run.

PAINTING TIPS

• Squeeze out only a small amount of paint at a time and cover leftover paint with a piece of plastic wrap.

• Rinse your brushes right away and change the water frequently, or some colors may look dirty.

• Paint dark colors over light ones and allow paint to dry between colors.

• When mixing colors, start with the lighter color and add the darker one a bit at a time.

• Papier-mâché surfaces are usually bumpy, so painting details can be difficult. Use big, bold designs.

SPONGING

Sponge painting is a fast way to create texture and layer colors. Dip a small piece of sponge into the paint, then dab it on your surface.

DRY BRUSHING

Dry-brush painting adds another color while still letting the first show through. Dab a dry brush into the paint, wipe most of the paint off the brush onto the palette, then very lightly paint the surface of your piece.

DECORATING

• When the piece is painted, glue on decorations such as feathers, sparkles, pipe cleaners, wool scraps, roly eyes or anything else you want.

• Another way to finish your piece is to use small squares of colored paper, tissue, wrapping paper, colored comics, blank newsprint or white paper as the final layer of papier-mâché. You can decorate a white piece using colored markers, pencils or crayons.

Fun frog

*This frog is eggsactly the right
project to make today!*

YOU WILL NEED

- papier-mâché supplies and goo
  (pages 4 – 6)
- an egg, a needle and a bowl
- aluminum foil
- thin cardboard
- 6 twist ties
- painting supplies (pages 10 – 11)

1 With the needle, carefully poke a hole in each end of the egg. Blow through one hole so that the liquid squirts out the other hole into the bowl. Gently rinse and dry the egg.

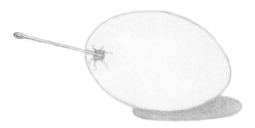

2 For the eyeballs, crumple up two 10 cm (4 in.) squares of foil into balls and flatten them on one side.

3 Draw two feet and two hands on the cardboard and cut them out. Trace around each once and cut out the shapes.

4 For each leg, twist two twist ties together and glue one end to a foot. Glue the other foot on top.

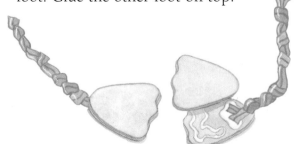

5 For each arm, fold one twist tie in half, twist it together, and glue one end to a hand. Glue the other hand on top.

6 Glue the eyeballs, arms and legs to the body. Secure them with tape. For a sitting frog, gently flatten the bottom of the egg and tape over the crushed part.

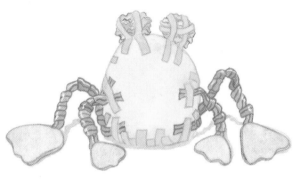

7 Cover the frog with four layers of papier-mâché and let them dry.

8 Gently sand the frog smooth, apply gesso and paint.

LUCKY PIG

You need five foil balls (four feet, one snout), two ears (see "Adding on parts" on page 9) and one twist tie.

Glue the ears, feet and snout to the egg, then cover with papier-mâché.

Fold the twist-tie tail in half and cover it with papier-mâché. Wind the tail around a pencil to curl it.

When everything is dry, poke a hole in the pig's bottom and glue in the tail, then sand, apply gesso and paint.

Giraffe pencil holder

This holder is great for storing pens and pencils that keep rolling off your desk or hiding under notebooks.

YOU WILL NEED

- papier-mâché supplies and goo (pages 4 – 6)
- a clean, empty cardboard frozen-juice container
- corrugated cardboard
- painting supplies (pages 10 – 11)
- wool (optional)

1 Lightly sand the juice container to remove the shine, so that the papier-mâché will stick properly.

2 Draw a giraffe's head on the cardboard and cut it out. Trace around the head twice and cut out the shapes. Draw two ears and two horns on the cardboard and cut them out.

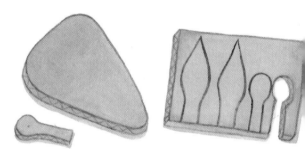

3 Glue the ears and horns to one head piece. Secure them with tape. Glue the other two head pieces on top of the first, so that the ears and horns are between the layers.

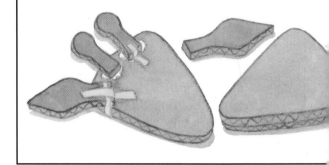

4 Cut eight leg strips out of cardboard, each about 2.5 cm x 15 cm (1 in. x 6 in.). Glue two strips together for each leg, then glue the legs to the bottom of the container. Secure them with tape.

5 Cut three neck strips out of cardboard, each about 2.5 cm x 15 cm (1 in. x 6 in.). Cut 1 cm (½ in.) off one strip and 2 cm (¾ in.) off another. Place the strips together so that they are even at one end and staggered at the other. Glue the strips together, leaving 5 cm (2 in.) of the even end unglued.

6 Glue the head to the staggered end of the neck so that it sticks out a bit. Secure it with tape.

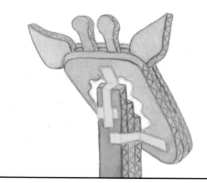

7 Slip the unglued part of the neck over the top of the container with two layers inside and one outside. Glue it in place and secure with tape.

8 Cover the giraffe with four layers of papier-mâché and let them dry.

9 Gently sand the giraffe smooth, apply gesso and paint. If you want, braid some wool for a tail and glue it in place.

Cat and mouse bookends

Keep the mouse safe by placing your books between this pair.

YOU WILL NEED

- papier-mâché supplies and goo (pages 4 – 6)
- 2 small, empty juice boxes
- sand, stones or anything heavy
- corrugated cardboard
- painting supplies (pages 10 – 11)
- pipe cleaners or wool
- cork pads (optional)

1 Lightly sand the boxes to remove the shine. Fill them with sand or stones and tape them closed.

2 Draw cat and mouse heads on the cardboard and cut them out. Trace around each and cut out the shapes, then glue the layers together.

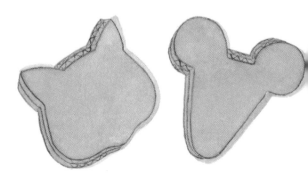

3 Draw eight paws about 5 cm (2 in.) long on the cardboard and cut them out. Draw two noses on the cardboard and cut them out.

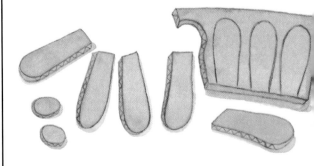

4 Cover all the pieces and the boxes with four layers of papier-mâché and let them dry.

5 Glue the paws to the bottom of the boxes and let them dry.

6 Glue the noses to the heads, then glue a head to the front of each box. To make the mouse head stick out, glue and tape a small piece of folded cardboard in between the head and the box. Let the glue dry. Add two layers of papier-mâché to attach the heads and the paws securely to the boxes.

7 Gently sand the cat and mouse smooth, apply gesso and paint.

8 Braid pipe cleaners or wool for tails and glue them in place. Glue pipe cleaner whiskers on the mouse.

9 To prevent slipping, you can glue cork pads to the bottom.

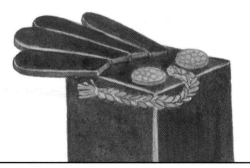

Handy hound

This watchdog keeps track of your keys, necklace or watch.

YOU WILL NEED

- papier-mâché supplies and goo (pages 4 – 6)
- corrugated cardboard
- a small metal hook
- 5 cm (2 in.) length of ½ in. dowel
- painting supplies (pages 10 – 11)
- string or ribbon

1 Draw a head on the cardboard and cut it out. Trace around it and cut out the shape, then glue the pieces together.

2 Draw a body on the cardboard and cut it out. Trace around it and cut out the shape, then glue the pieces together.

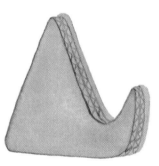

3 Draw two front paws, one hind paw, one nose and one collar on the cardboard and cut them out.

4 Screw the hook into the middle of the dowel. Glue the dowel to the collar and secure it with tape.

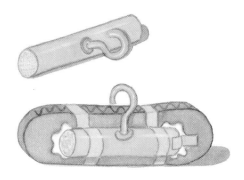

5 Cover all the pieces except the hook with four layers of papier-mâché and let them dry. Bend the ears before drying (see page 8).

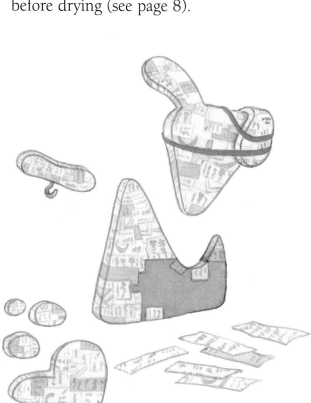

6 Glue the collar and the paws to the body. Glue the head to the neck, with the tip of the snout glued to the collar. Glue the nose to the head.

7 Secure the head with tape. Add two layers of papier-mâché to attach the parts securely to the body. Let them dry.

8 Gently sand the dog smooth, apply gesso and paint. Tie a string or ribbon around the neck to hang up your hound.

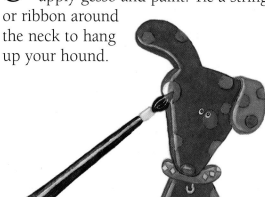

Bug vase

Flowers keep this bug happily buzzing.

YOU WILL NEED

- papier-mâché supplies and goo
  (pages 4 – 6)
- a clean glass bottle with a long neck
- aluminum foil
- thin cardboard
- painting supplies (pages 10 – 11)
- acrylic varnish (optional)
- 4 pipe cleaners

1 Cover the bottle with four layers of papier-mâché and let them dry.

2 For the eyeballs, crumple up two 10 cm (4 in.) squares of foil into balls and flatten them on one side. Cover with four layers of papier-mâché and let them dry.

3 Cut out a 2 cm x 5 cm (¾ in. x 2 in.) strip of cardboard for the nose. Fold the strip in thirds lengthwise and tape it to hold. Bend the strip into an **L** shape, then glue and tape the short end to the neck of the bottle, about 1 cm (½ in.) from the top. Cover the nose with four layers of papier-mâché and let them dry.

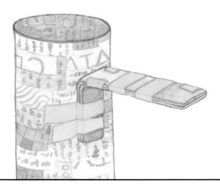

4 Glue the eyeballs to the bottle, then add two layers of papier-mâché to attach them securely. Let them dry.

5 Draw four wings on the cardboard and cut them out. Trace around each wing once and cut out the shapes. Glue the layers together, leaving 1 cm (½ in.) along the small straight edge unglued. Fold out the unglued parts, glue the wings to the bottle, and secure them with tape. Cover the wings with four layers of papier-mâché and let them dry.

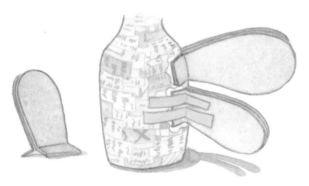

6 If you like, draw a bow tie on the cardboard and cut it out. Cover with four layers of papier-mâché and let them dry.

7 Gently sand the bug smooth, apply gesso and paint. If you plan to use water in the vase, apply three coats of acrylic varnish, letting it dry between coats. Otherwise, put dried flowers in your vase.

8 Cut the pipe cleaners in half and curl one end of each piece into a flat spiral the size of a dime. Glue the spirals to the vase for legs and antennae. Bend into position. Glue the bow tie to the neck.

Lion magazine holder

The king of the jungle will guard your favorite magazines.

YOU WILL NEED

- papier-mâché supplies and goo (pages 4 – 6)
- a clean shoe box or small detergent box without lid
- corrugated cardboard
- painting supplies (pages 10 – 11)

1 Lightly sand the box to remove any shine. Cover it inside and out with four layers of papier-mâché and let them dry.

2 Draw two haunches on the cardboard and cut them out. Trace around each twice and cut out the shapes. Glue the three layers together.

3 Draw two front paws about 13 cm (5 in.) long on the cardboard and cut them out. Trace around each twice and cut out the shapes. Cut 4 cm (1 ½ in.) off four of the paws. Glue three pieces together for each paw so that the rounded front is even and the longer piece is on the bottom.

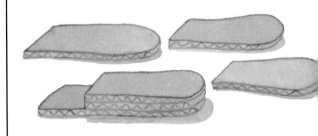

4 Draw the mane on the cardboard and cut it out.

5 Draw a head, two ears, a nose and a tail on the cardboard and cut them out. Trace around the tail only and cut it out, then glue the layers together.

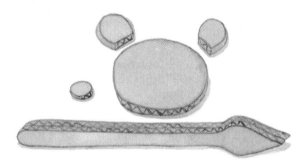

6 Cover all the parts with four layers of papier-mâché. Curl some of the mane points, so that not all of them are flat. Curve the tail around the box. Let everything dry.

7 Glue and tape the pieces to the box in the following order:
- the front paws, with the longer piece glued to the bottom of the box
- the haunches to the sides
- the tail to the back and around one side
- the mane to the front
- the ears to the mane
- the head to the mane
- the nose to the head

8 Cover the joints with two layers of papier-mâché and let them dry.

9 Gently sand the lion smooth, apply gesso and paint.

Money-muncher fish

Remember to feed your fish daily — but only with coins.

YOU WILL NEED

- papier-mâché supplies and goo (pages 4 – 6)
- a balloon
- string
- thin cardboard
- painting supplies (pages 10 – 11)

1 Blow up the balloon to about 13 cm (5 in.) in diameter and knot it. Tie a string around the knot.

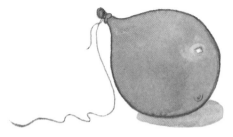

2 Tape the knotted end of the balloon to your work surface. Cover the balloon, but not the knot, with five layers of papier-mâché. Hang the balloon from the string to dry.

3 Repeat step 2 two or three times, so that the shape will be solid. If there are any soft spots, add more papier-mâché.

4 Pull the balloon out of the papier-mâché by tugging at the knot and popping the balloon.

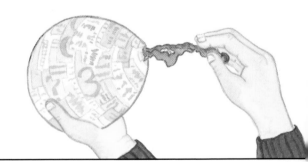

5 Ask an adult to cut a mouth slot in the papier-mâché about 1 cm x 4 cm (½ in. x 1 ½ in.), so that coins fit in and out easily. To remove coins, hold the fish with the slot facing down, insert a butter knife, then shake until the coins slip out.

7 Draw a tail and two side fins on the cardboard and cut them out. Trace around each shape and cut them out. Glue the pieces together, leaving 1 cm (½ in.) unglued along the straight edges.

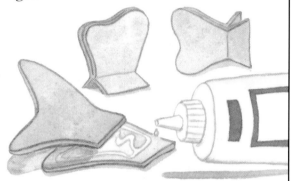

8 Fold out the unglued parts of the tail and fins. Position the tail and the side fins so that the fish doesn't roll. Glue them to the body and secure with tape. Glue and tape the dorsal fin to the top.

6 Draw a dorsal fin on the cardboard and cut it out. The bottom edge should be slightly curved so it will fit on the round body. Trace around the fin and cut it out. Glue the pieces together, leaving 1 cm (½ in.) unglued along the bottom edge. Cut 1 cm (½ in.) deep slits along the bottom edge at 1 cm (½ in.) intervals.

9 Cover with four layers of papier-mâché and let them dry.

10 Gently sand the fish smooth, apply gesso and paint.

Elephant box

A box for storing special memories.
Remember, elephants never forget!
If you want to simplify this project,
make it without the bird.

YOU WILL NEED

- papier-mâché supplies and goo
  (pages 4 – 6)
- a large round cardboard container
  with a cardboard lid, such as
  an ice cream container
- corrugated cardboard and thin cardboard
- aluminum foil
- a twist tie
- painting supplies (pages 10 – 11)
- ribbon

1 Lightly sand the container and the lid inside and out to remove any shine. Cover them, inside and out, with four layers of papier-mâché. Put only two layers around the rim of the container and inside the lid's brim, or the lid may not fit. Let them dry.

Tip: If you have an extra lid, let the container dry with it on. That way, the container will stay round. Once the outside is dry, remove the lid so that the inside can dry.

2 Cut eight leg strips out of corrugated cardboard, each about 4 cm x 30 cm (1 ½ in. x 12 in.). For each leg, roll up one strip, secure it with tape, then roll another strip around it and tape the end. Cover the legs with four layers of papier-mâché and let them dry.

3 Glue the legs to the bottom of the container and secure them with tape.

4 Draw a trunk on the corrugated cardboard and cut it out. Trace around it twice and cut out the shapes. From the top end, cut 1 cm (½ in.) off one piece and 2 cm (¾ in.) off another. Glue the pieces together so that the bottom ends are even and the top is staggered.

5 Glue the staggered end of the trunk to the container at least 5 cm (2 in.) below the top, so that it sticks out a bit. Secure it with tape.

6 Draw two tusks on the corrugated cardboard and cut them out. Trace around each piece once and cut out the shapes. Glue the pieces together, leaving 1 cm (½ in.) unglued along the straight edges. When the glue is dry, fold out the flaps, then glue the tusks to the container. Secure them with tape.

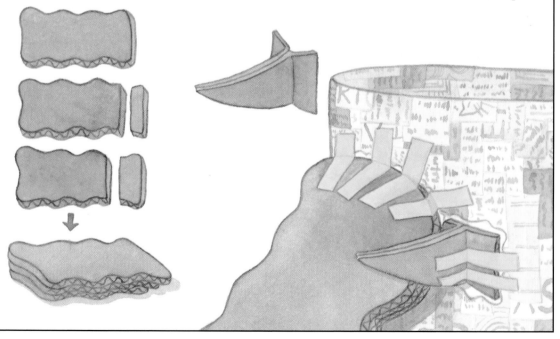

Instructions continue on the next page ☞

7 Draw two ears on the thin cardboard and cut them out. Trace around each piece once and cut out the shapes. Glue the pieces together, leaving 1 cm (½ in.) unglued along the straight edges. When the glue is dry, fold out the flaps, then glue them to the container at least 2.5 cm (1 in.) below the top. Secure them with tape.

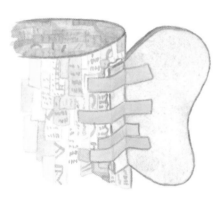

8 Cover the elephant's ears, trunk and tusks with four layers of papier-mâché. Join the legs to the body with two layers of papier-mâché. Gently shape the ears by curving the top and the bottom. Let everything dry.

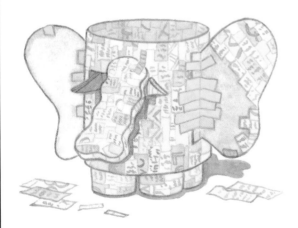

9 For the bird, wrap some foil around the twist tie to form an egg-shaped ball about 2.5 cm (1 in.) high. The twist tie should stick out of the bottom. Cover the foil, but not the twist tie, with four layers of papier-mâché and let them dry.

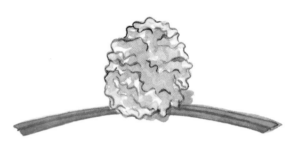

10 Poke two small holes about 2 cm (¾ in.) apart in the center of the lid. You may have to cut off the bottom of the bird's body so that it sits flat on the lid. Cover the bottom of the bird with glue, then slip the ends of the twist tie through the holes and twist them together inside the lid. Tape the twist tie to the lid, then cover the tape with papier-mâché. Add a few small strips of papier-mâché to secure the bird to the lid. Let them dry.

11 Cut out a diamond-shaped beak from thin cardboard. Cover it with three layers of papier-mâché, then bend the beak in half and let it dry.

12 Glue the beak to the front of the body. You may have to make a slight indentation in the body first, so that the beak stays in place. Let the glue dry.

13 Cut out two wings from thin cardboard. Trace around them, cut out the shapes, and glue the layers together. Glue the wings to the sides of the body.

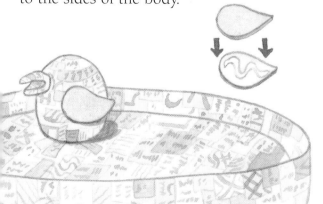

14 Gently sand the elephant and lid smooth, apply gesso and paint. Try sponge painting, if you like.

15 Glue ribbon inside the brim of the lid to prevent the lid from sticking.

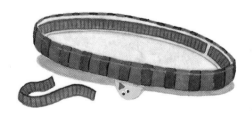

Alligator box

This alligator is a secret box for storing small treasures. The little birds are adorable, but optional.

YOU WILL NEED

- papier-mâché supplies and goo (pages 4 – 6)
- a toilet paper roll
- a paper towel roll
- aluminum foil
- thin cardboard and corrugated cardboard
- masking tape and duct tape
- painting supplies (pages 10 – 11)
- ribbon

1 Cut out two triangles about 8 cm (3 in.) long from one end of each roll. Trim the ends into a point.

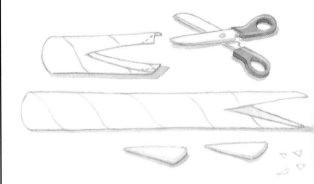

2 Tape the cut sides of the toilet paper roll together and stuff it with crumpled newspaper.

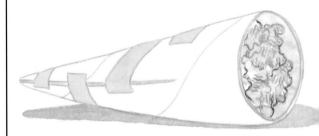

3 Tape the uncut ends of the two rolls together.

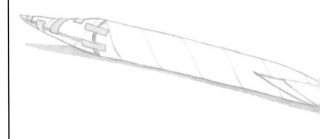

4 Draw an oval opening on the top of the paper towel roll about 4 cm x 18 cm (1 ½ in. x 7 in.). Ask an adult to cut out the oval lid carefully with a craft knife. Set the lid aside.

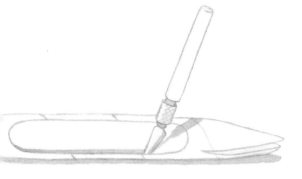

5 Cut out two corrugated cardboard circles that fit inside the paper towel roll. Tape them inside to block the mouth and tail openings.

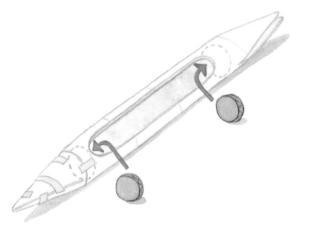

6 Draw two front and two hind legs on the corrugated cardboard and cut them out. Trace around each piece once and cut out the shapes, then glue the pieces together. Bend the legs at the ankles, making sure to have two right and two left legs.

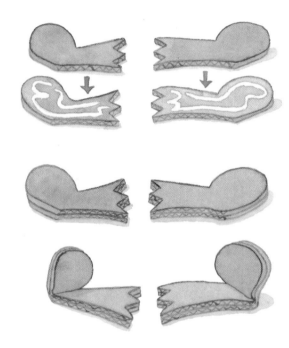

7 Crumple up two 10 cm (4 in.) squares of foil into balls for eyes. Make two much smaller balls for nostrils.

Instructions continue on the next page ☞

8 Glue the eyeballs, nostrils and legs to the body and secure them with masking tape. Cover the alligator and the lid with four layers of papier-mâché and let them dry.

9 Draw four teeth on cardboard and cut them out. Trace around each tooth once and cut out the shapes. Glue the layers together, leaving 0.5 cm (¼ in.) unglued. Fold this part out and glue the flaps to the inside of the mouth. Cover the teeth with three layers of papier-mâché and let them dry.

10 Use duct tape to attach the lid to the box along the inside. Close it to see if the lid fits. Lightly sand the tape, then cover it — except at the part that hinges — with three layers of papier-mâché. Let them dry.

11 For each bird, crumple up one 10 cm (4 in.) and one 8 cm (3 in.) square of foil into two balls. Cover with four layers of papier-mâché, let them dry, then glue them together.

12 Draw a beak, a tail and two wings on thin cardboard and cut them out. Trace around the wings once, cut them out, and glue the layers together.

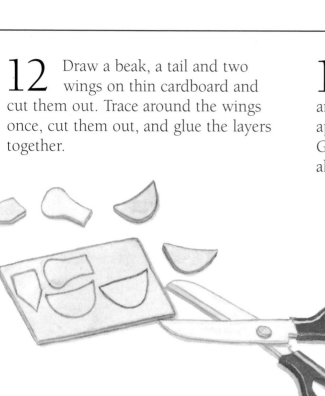

13 Glue the beak to the head and the tail to the body. Cover the beak and the tail with three layers of papier-mâché and let them dry. Glue the wings to the body.

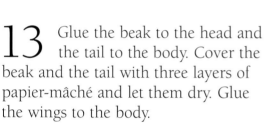

14 Gently sand the alligator and the birds smooth, apply gesso and paint. Glue the birds to the alligator.

15 Glue the ribbon inside the box, so that it covers the duct-tape hinge.

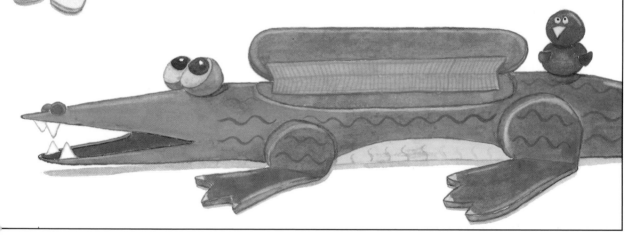

Garbage gobbler

This is one dinosaur that will thrive in our world. Feed it paper garbage only.

YOU WILL NEED

- papier-mâché supplies and goo (pages 4 – 6)
- a large cardboard detergent box about 27 cm (11 in.) high
- thin cardboard and corrugated cardboard
- masking tape and duct tape
- aluminum foil
- painting supplies (pages 10 – 11)
- ribbon
- acrylic varnish (optional)

1 Strengthen the hinge where the lid is joined to the box with a strip of duct tape along the outside and inside. Check that the lid still opens and closes.

2 Cut out two triangles from corrugated cardboard for the snout. The bottom edge should be about as wide as the box. Make one triangle 15 cm (6 in.) longer. Trace around each triangle once and cut out the shapes. Glue the layers together.

3 Glue the longer triangle to the top of the lid. Fold the bottom edge of the other triangle under 2.5 cm (1 in.) and glue it to the front of the box 2.5 cm (1 in.) below the rim. Secure them with masking tape and check that the lid still closes.

4 For the belly, crumple up some newspaper pages and tape them to the front of the box with masking tape. You may need someone to help with this.

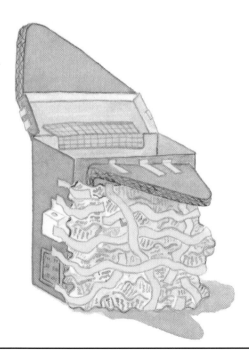

5 Crumple up some newspaper and tape it to the sides and back of the box to hide the box shape. Also tape some to the top and bottom of the snout and to the top of the lid to round out the head. Be sure that the lid still opens.

6 Cut out a long curved pointed tail from corrugated cardboard. Trace around it once and cut out the shape. Glue the layers together, then glue the straight end to the bottom of the box. Secure it with masking tape. Squish the tail a bit so that it isn't flat.

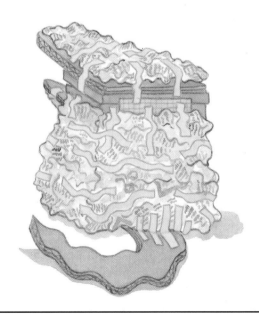

Instructions continue on the next page ☞

7 Cut out different-sized triangles from corrugated cardboard for head and tail spikes. Trace around each once and cut them out. Glue the layers together, leaving 1 cm (½ in.) unglued along the bottom edges. Fold this part out, then glue the triangles to the head and along the back and the tail. Secure them with masking tape and check that the lid still opens.

8 Cover everything, inside and out, with five layers of papier-mâché, but put only two layers around the rim of the box. The lid may no longer close perfectly. Leave it open to dry.

9 For the eyes, crumple up two 30 cm (12 in.) squares of foil into balls and flatten them on one side. Glue them to the head and secure them with masking tape.

10 Cut teeth from thin cardboard. Trace around each tooth once and cut out the shapes. Glue the teeth together, leaving 1 cm (½ in.) unglued. Fold this part out, glue the flaps to the inside of the mouth, and secure them with masking tape.

11 Cover the teeth, eyeballs and the rest of the body with four layers of papier-mâché and let them dry.

12 Cut two haunches and two arms from corrugated cardboard. Trace around each piece once and cut out the shapes. Glue the layers together.

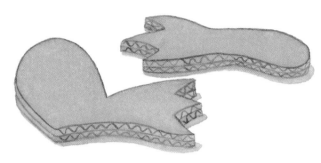

13 Bend the feet at the ankles so that the feet lie flat, and secure them with masking tape. Crumple up some foil (or newspaper) and tape it to one side only of each piece. Make sure you have left and right arms and legs. Bend the arms slightly so that they curve around the body.

14 Cover the arms and haunches with at least four layers of papier-mâché and let them dry.

15 Glue the arms and haunches to the body and secure them with tape. Fill in any gaps between the body and the haunches or shoulders with crumpled-up newspaper. Reinforce with four layers of papier-mâché and let them dry.

16 Gently sand the garbage gobbler smooth, apply gesso and paint. Glue the ribbon around the inside brim of the lid to prevent the paint from sticking.

17 Varnish the inside to protect it, if you like.

Bird bowl

This wacky bird is perfect for snacks.
Line it with a napkin, because
it can't be washed.

YOU WILL NEED

- papier-mâché supplies and goo
  (pages 4 – 6)
- a bowl (small or medium, glass or plastic)
- petroleum jelly and paper towels
- thin cardboard and corrugated cardboard
- 2 toilet paper rolls
- 18 twist ties
- painting supplies (pages 10 – 11)
- acrylic varnish (optional)

1 Grease the inside of the bowl with petroleum jelly. This will make it easier to remove the papier-mâché bowl later. Cover the inside of the bowl with five layers of papier-mâché. Smooth the strips so that they take the form of the bowl. Let the papier-mâché dry in the bowl.

2 Gently ease the papier-mâché out of the bowl. You may need to loosen it by carefully running a butter knife around the rim. Wipe off the petroleum jelly from the papier-mâché bowl with a paper towel.

3 Add four more layers of papier-mâché to the outside of the papier-mâché bowl, then let them dry. Repeat this step once or twice. When dry, trim the rim with scissors.

4 Draw tail feathers on the thin cardboard and cut them out. Trace around each feather twice, then cut out the shapes. Glue three pieces together for each feather, leaving the bottom 4 cm (1½ in.) unglued.

5 Slip the unglued part of the feathers over the rim of the bowl with two layers outside and one inside. Glue them in place and secure with tape.

6 For the neck, cut out two strips of thin cardboard 2.5 cm (1 in.) wide and three times the height of your bowl. Glue them together, leaving 8 cm (3 in.) at each end unglued. Slip one unglued end over the rim of the bowl, glue it in place, and secure with tape. Bend the strips 9 cm (3½ in.) from the other end. Cut the ends to a point for the beak.

7 Cut two triangles 8 cm (3 in.) long from a toilet paper roll, for the beak. Tape them to the neck strips — one on top and one underneath. Stuff some crumpled paper into the gap.

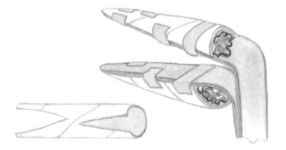

8 Tape some crumpled paper to the top of the head to make it round.

9 Cut open the other toilet paper roll and wrap it around the neck. You may have to cut the roll to fit. Secure it with tape.

Instructions continue on the next page ☞

10 Cover the beak, head, neck and tail feathers with four layers of papier-mâché and let them dry. Curve the tail feathers before drying.

11 Draw two wings on the corrugated cardboard and cut them out. Cover the wings with four layers of papier-mâché, curve them slightly and let them dry.

12 Twist three twist ties together for each toe, then tape three toes together at one end and shape the foot. Cover the feet with four layers of papier-mâché and let them dry.

13 Glue the wings to the sides of the bowl. Glue the feet to the bottom so that they stick out and stabilize the bowl. Add three layers of papier-mâché to join the feet to the bowl and let them dry.

14 Gently sand the bird smooth, apply gesso and paint.

15 Varnish the bowl to protect it, if you like.